PROGRESSIVE

HARMONICA

for
Young Beginners

by William Lee Johnson
Illustrated by James Stewart

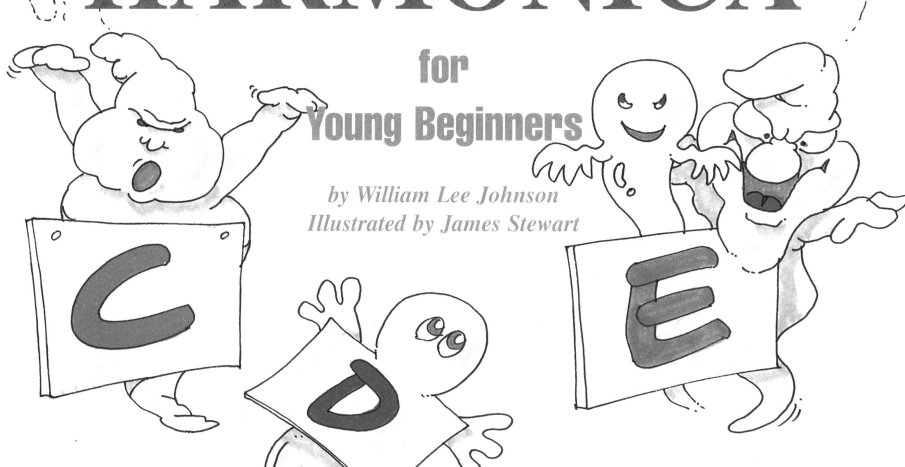

Introduction

Progressive *Harmonica* Method for young beginners has been designed to introduce the younger student to the basics of harmonica playing and reading music. To maximize the students' enjoyment and interest, the Progressive Young Beginner series incorporates an extensive repertoire of well-known children's songs. All the songs have been carefully graded into an easy-to-follow, lesson-by-lesson format, which assumes no prior knowledge of music or the harmonica by the student.

This book contains easy arrangements involving five notes (C, D, E, F and G). A combination of harmonica tablature and standard music notation is provided for each song. This will allow ease of playing while learning standard notation, incorporating quarter, half, dotted, and whole notes and their equivalent rests. The student is also introduced to basic terms such as barlines, repeat signs, and lead-in notes. New pieces of information are highlighted by color boxes, and color illustrations are used throughout to stimulate and maintain the student's interest.

Let's Practice Together

We have recorded all the songs in this book onto a CD. When your teacher's not there, instead of practicing by yourself, you can play along with us. Playing will be much more fun, and you will learn faster. On the recording each song is played twice.

- The first time contains the song with the accompaniment.
- The second time contains just the accompaniment.
- A drum is used to begin each exercise and to help you keep time.

Note to Teachers: "Key of C" Harmonica

The CD is tuned for use with the most common type of harmonica available, the **diatonic** or **Major-Tuned** ten hole harmonica in the key of **C**. If the student will be utilizing the CD in conjunction with the book, this type of harmonica **must** be used.

Contents

Lesson 1

Parts of Harmonica

This is your harmonica!
Shown below are the parts of your harmonica.
The holes and the hole numbers are the most important parts to know.

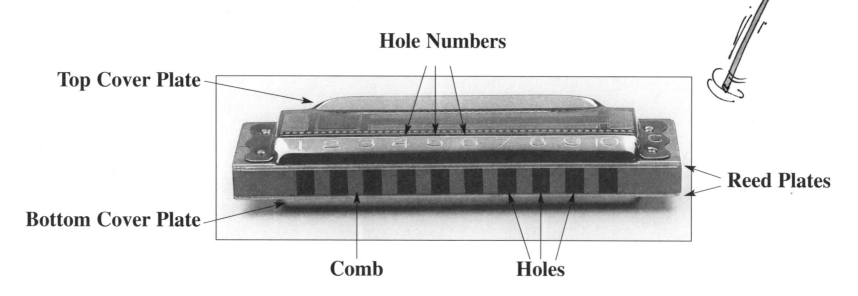

Hole Numbers

Top Cover Plate

Reed Plates

Bottom Cover Plate

Comb   **Holes**

Things to Remember
1. Your harmonica has ten holes.
2. Each hole has a number.
3. The top side of your harmonica is the side with the numbers from 1 to 10.

How to Hold the Harmonica

Hold your harmonica in your **left** hand.
Your thumb should be on the bottom. Your four fingers should be on top.
Keep all four fingers of your left hand straight, and pressed gently but closely together.

Look at the two pictures to see that you are holding your harmonica correctly.

Don't squeeze your harmonica too tightly or your hand will get tired.

How to Make Sounds on the Harmonica

Hold the harmonica in your left hand.
Breathe gently through any of the holes.
Do not worry about which holes you are breathing through.
You can make a sound by **inhaling** through the holes.
Or you can make a sound by **exhaling** through the holes.

A Lip Lesson

Your harmonica should be in-between your lips when you play.
Your upper lip should be just a little bit on top of the top cover plate.
Your lower lip should be just a little bit under the bottom cover plate.
Make sure that air can not escape from the corners of your mouth when you breathe through your harmonica.

How to Play "Chords" on the Harmonica

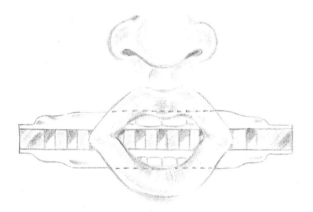

Begin by covering about three holes with your mouth at one time.
Your mouth should be about as wide open as it is when you are talking.
Playing three holes at once is called playing a **chord**.

Low Sounds, Middle Sounds, High Sounds

The holes with **low** numbers make **low** sounds.
The holes with **high** numbers make **high** sounds.
The holes in the **middle** make **in-between** sounds.

Same Holes, Different Sounds

Cover any three holes with your mouth.
Inhale through those holes.

Now exhale through those holes.

You will hear one chord when you **inhale**, and a different chord when you **exhale**.

Hordes of Chords

Now play lots of chords. Inhale and exhale through your harmonica.
Play some low chords. Play some high chords. Play some chords in the middle.

Lesson 2

How Much Air to Use

Use as much air as you would use when you are talking.
Breathing too hard is not good for your harmonica.
It may not be good for people who are listening either.

What to Do with Your Nose

Try not to let air in or out through your nose while you play.
Practice breathing through your mouth only.

Music Notes

Your harmonica was built to produce chords very easily.
Whenever you cover three holes and breathe, you will play a chord.
Your harmonica can also play **notes**.
When you cover just one hole and breathe, you will play a note.

You can play a note by inhaling or exhaling.

The Musical Alphabet

There are only seven letters used for notes in music. these notes are know as the **musical alphabet**. They are: **A B C D E F G**

Soon you will learn how to play some of these seven notes on your harmonica. Then you will learn to read harmonica music.

Two Ways of Playing Notes

You must cover one hole at a time to play notes. There are two ways to play notes on the harmonica. The **Pucker Method** is very easy. That is the way you will learn. The other way is harder. The hard way is called **Tongue-blocking**. You will study tongue-blocking in a more advanced book.

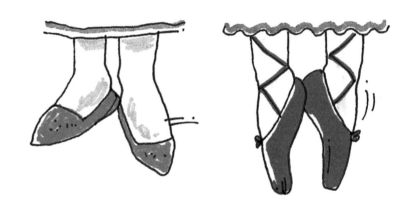

A Warning to Beginning Harmonica Players and Their Teachers

Playing only one hole at a time takes practice. Most beginners need a few weeks of practice to play one hole at a time. But harmonica players are lucky. Even when we accidentally cover more than one hole at a time, it still sounds fine. We are just playing a chord instead of a note.

Very Important:
Please practice playing one hole at a time. But go on to the other lessons even if you can not play one hole at a time yet.

The "Pucker" Method of Playing Notes

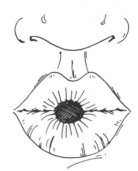

This is the easiest way to play notes.

Pucker your lips to mike a small, round hole. This is what you do when you drink through a straw, or when you whistle.

Make sure thar your upper lip is still a little bit on top of the harmonica. Make sure that your lower lip is still a little bit under the harmonica.

Playing Notes on Hole Number 1

Look carefully at your harmonica. Aim your lips at the hole number **1**.

Cover hole number **1** with your lips puckered.

Make sure that your lips are directly over hole number **1**.

Exhale through hole number **1**. This note is called a **C** note.

Now inhale through hole number **1**. This note is called a **D** note.

Playing a Note on Hole Number 2

Now move your lips a little higher, and aim at hole number **2**.

Exhale through hole number **2**. This note is called an **E** note. Don't try the **2** inhale yet.

The Note Middle C

Pucker your lips and exhale through hole number **2**.

Now make your lips wide and exhale though holes number **1**, **2** and **3**.

Now try the pucker again. It sounds fine whichever way you do it!

Playing Other Notes

Now you are ready to start learning to play notes on any hole.
Pucker your lips and choose **any** hole.
Aim your lips a that hole and exhale. You will play a note.

Keep your lips over the same hole and inhale.
You will play a different note from the same hole.

Can you play the two notes of the hole number **4**?
How about the two notes of the hole number **5**? Number **7**?
How about hole number **10**?

Notes We will Use

Some notes are easier to play and some are harder.
In this book we will use five easy notes in the middle of the harmonica.
The number **2** hole is hard to breathe in on. The highest notes can be squeaky.
You will learn to play these harder notes in a more advanced book.

Lesson 3

An Easy Way to Know Which Hole to Play

Harmonica tablature is a very easy way to know which note to play on the harmonica. Soon, harmonica tablature will help us learn how to read music.

Harmonica tablature gives you a **number** for each note.
This number tells you which hole to cover with your lips.
If you see a number **4**, you will cover hole number **4** with your lips.
Harmonica tablature also tells you whether to **inhale** or to **exhale** on that hole.
If you see an **e** next to a number, you will exhale on that hole number.
If you see an **i** next to a number, you will inhale on that hole number.

4e	4i
Exhale on hole number **4**	**Inhale** on hole number **4**

Now You Try It!

Look at the harmonica tablature and play the right note.
Hint: the pictures may help!

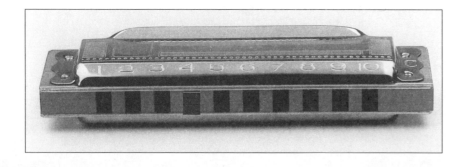

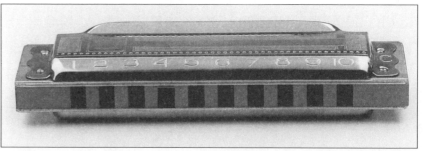

How to Read Music

Staff

These five lines are called the **staff** or **stave**. Music notes are written in the spaces and on the lines of the staff.

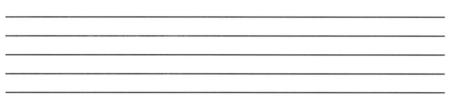

The Quarter Note

This is a musical note called a **quarter note**.

Treble Clef

This symbol is called a treble clef.
A staff with a treble clef written on it is called a **treble staff**.
Middle and high notes of the harmonica are played on the treble staff.
All of the harmonica music in this book will be written on the treble staff.

The Note C

Do you remember the names of the musical alphabet notes?

The Note C

The **C** note on your harmonica a little bit too low to fit on the staff.
The **C** note is written just below the treble staff on a short line (called a **leger line**).
This is what it looks like.

We play the **C** note by exhaling on hole number **4**.

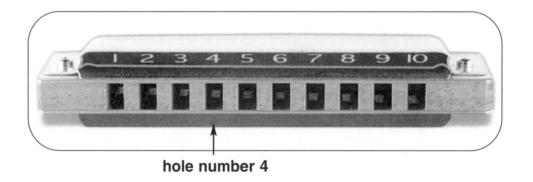

hole number 4

Here is a **C** note with harmonica tablature added.
The tablature will help you remember how to play this note.
Look at the staff and play one **C** note.

4e

The Quarter Rest

This symbol is called a **quarter rest**. It means that there is one count of silence.
Do not play any note. We place small counting numbers under rests.

 1. **Can You C?**

If your first song, called **Can you C?**, there are four **C** notes and four quarter rests. You will play one **C** note, then rest for one count.
Take a breath during the rest. The symbol (▼) will help remind you how to breathe **during the rest**.
On the recording there are four drumbeats to introduce this song.

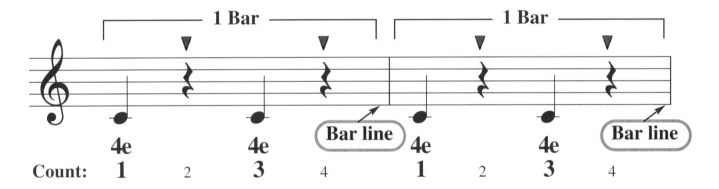

Bars

Music is divided into **bars** by **bar lines**. In your first song, **Can You C?**, there are two bars of music. As you play the notes and rests in each bar, try to count **1 2 3 4** in your head.

The Four Four Time Signature

 2.   Can You C a Rest?

In this song, you will have to play three **C** notes before resting. You will need to make **three little exhaled breaths** of air, one for each **C** note. Make sure that you have lots of air in your lungs when you begin. The symbol (▼) will help remind you how to breathe during the rests.

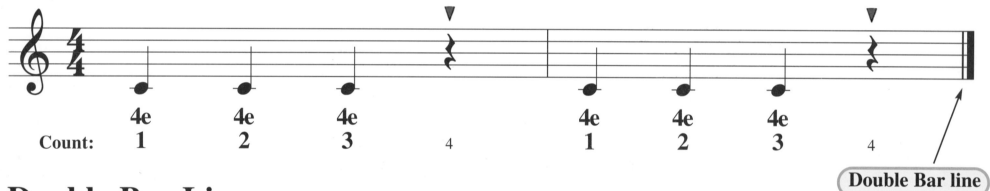

Count: 1   2   3   4   1   2   3   4

Double Bar line

Double Bar Line

The double bar line at the end of the song tells us that the song is finished.

Remember:
Do not worry if you cannot play one hole at a time yet. Simply make certain that you are aiming your lips at the correct hole and breathing correctly.
On the recording, the songs will be played once using single notes and then once using chords. You will find that they sound fine either way.

3. From C to C

The two dots at the end of this song are called a **repeat sign**. This means that you play the song again from the start.

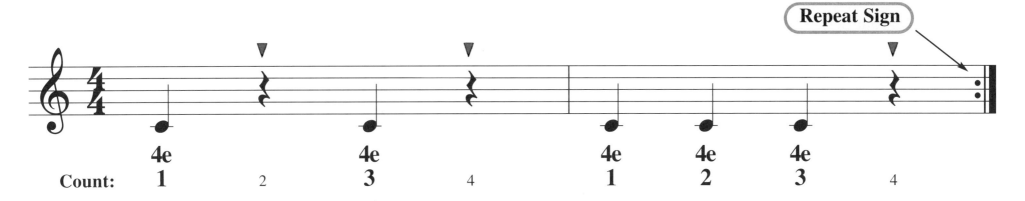

Repeat Sign

4e   4e   4e   4e   4e

Count: 1   2   3   4   1   2   3   4

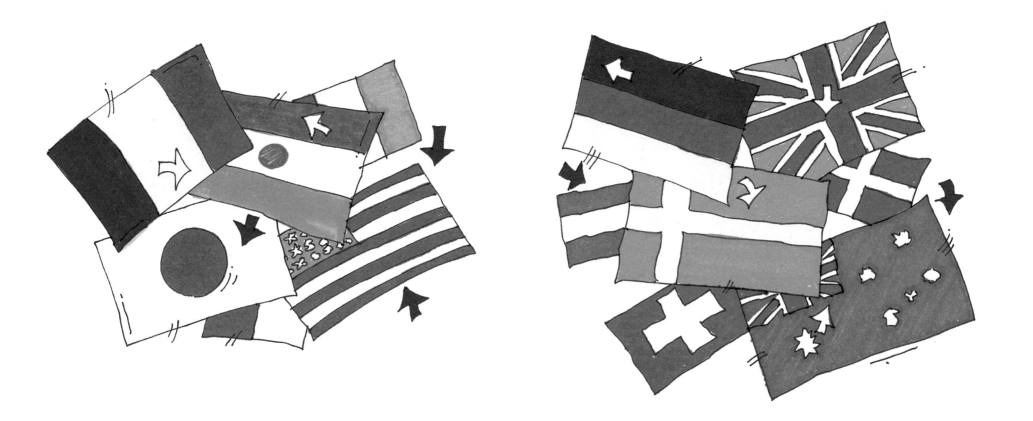

Lesson 4

The Note D

The Note D

The **D** note of your harmonica is written just below the bottom line of the treble staff. This is what it looks like.

4i

We play the **D** note by inhaling on hole number **4**.

 4.   D with Me

In this song, you will need to make **three little inhaled breaths**, one for each D note.
You will also need to **exhale** during the rests.

Do not exhale through your harmonica. Drop your jaw and exhale through your mouth under the harmonica. Keep your upper lip in place on top of the harmonica.
The symbol (ⱽ) will remind you to do this.

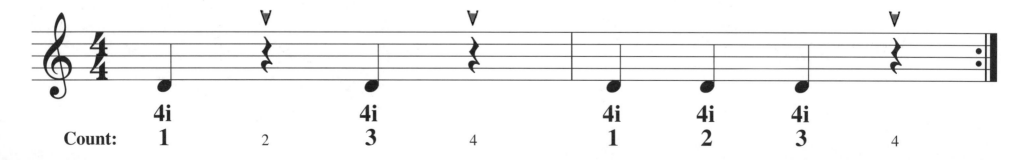

Count:	**4i**		**4i**		**4i**	**4i**	**4i**	
	1	2	**3**	4	**1**	**2**	**3**	4

5.   Play that CD

This song uses both notes **C** and **D** that you know.
Try to breathe through the harmonica except during the rests.

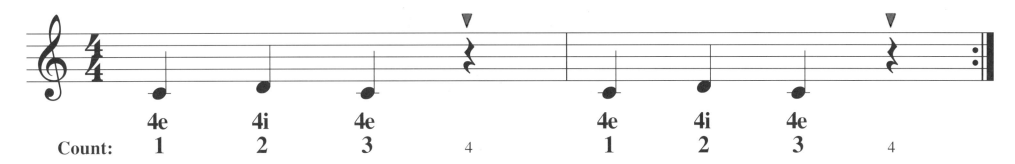

	4e	4i	4e		4e	4i	4e	
Count:	1	2	3	4	1	2	3	4

6.   Washington DC

This new song is four bars long. The letters above the staff, like **G** and **D** are **chord symbols**.
These tell other musicians what chords to play along with your music.

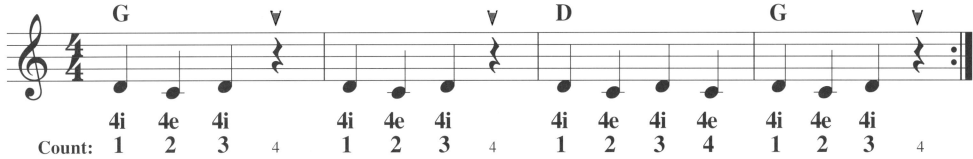

	4i	4e	4i		4i	4e	4i		4i	4e	4i	4e	4i	4e	4i	
Count:	1	2	3	4	1	2	3	4	1	2	3	4	1	2	3	4

The Note E

The **E** note on your harmonica is written on the bottom line of the treble staff. This is what it looks like. We play the **E** note by exhaling on hole number **5**.

 7.   E-Normous!

Take an enormous inhaled breath before playing the third bar of this song. If you need to, you can take a very quick breath in between notes.

5e

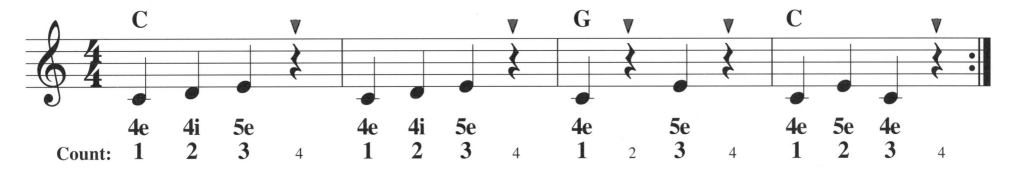

 8.   Slo and EZ CeeDee

9. EC Does It!

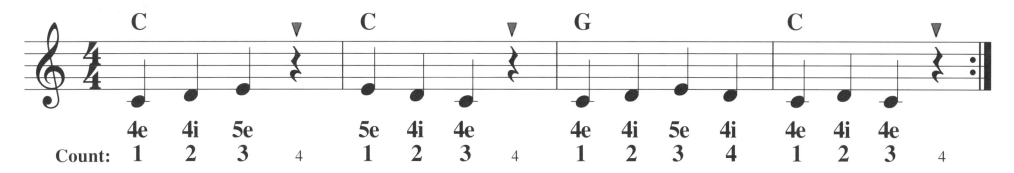

C — 4e(1) 4i(2) 5e(3) (4) | C — 5e(1) 4i(2) 4e(3) (4) | G — 4e(1) 4i(2) 5e(3) 4i(4) | C — 4e(1) 4i(2) 4e(3) (4)

Things to Remember

Moving quickly from one hole to another takes practice. Do not be discouraged if it seems difficult at first. Continue to work on your **pucker**. Try to obtain a single hole if possible. Even if you still can not obtain a single hole, go on to the next lessons.

Lesson 5

The Half Note

This symbol is a **half note**.
It lasts for two counts.
There are only two half notes in one bar of 𝄵 time.

Count: 1 2

The Half Rest

A black box sitting on the middle line of the staff is called a **half rest**.
It means **two** counts of silence.

Count: 1 2

 10.   Half Time

This song is **four** bars long. It contains half notes, using the notes **C, D** and **E** as well as a **half rest**.

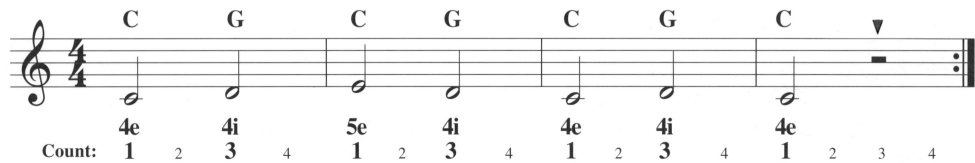

11. **Half a Loaf**

This song mixes half and quarter notes. It ends with three counts of silence (a half note rest plus a quarter note rest).

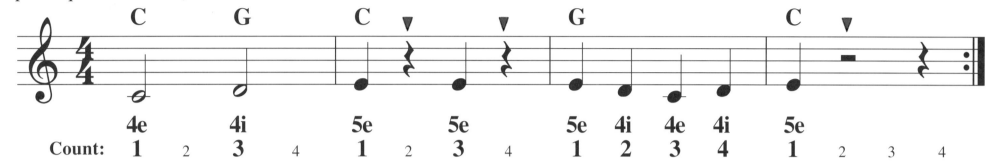

 12. **Not Half Bad**

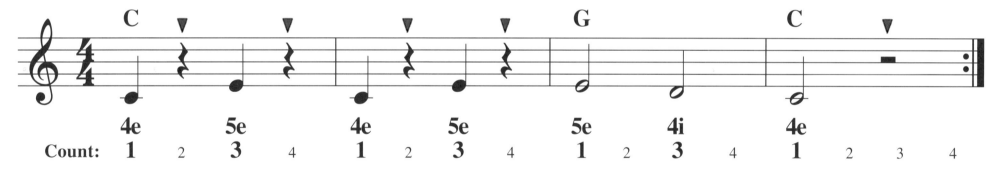

 13. **In the Light of the Moon**

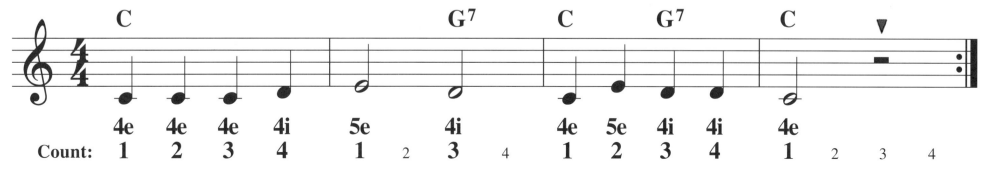

Traditional French

14. Merrily

This song is eight bars long. Each bar has been numbered.

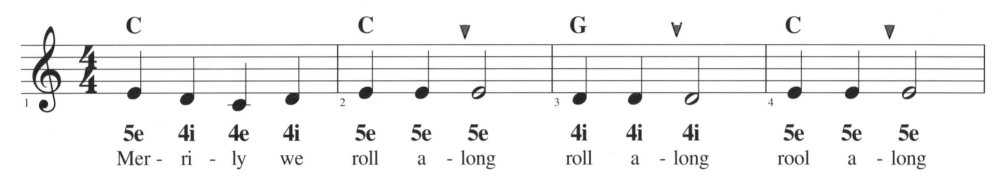

C				**C**			**G**			**C**		
5e	4i	4e	4i	5e	5e	5e	4i	4i	4i	5e	5e	5e
Mer -	ri -	ly	we	roll	a	- long	roll	a	- long	rool	a	- long

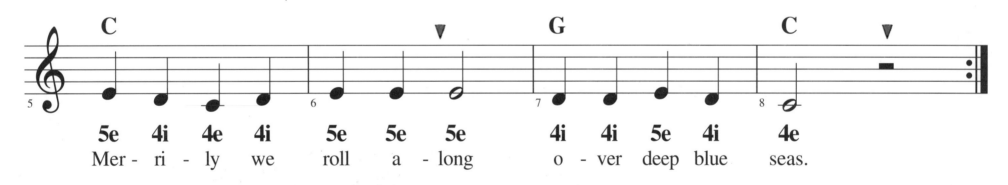

C							**G**			**C**	
5e	4i	4e	4i	5e	5e	5e	4i	4i	5e	4i	4e
Mer -	ri -	ly	we	roll	a	- long	o	- ver	deep	blue	seas.

Lesson 6

The Note F

The **F** note of your harmonica is written just above the bottom line of the treble staff.
Thus it is on the first space of the staff.
This is what it looks like.

We play the F note by **inhaling** on hole number **5**.

The Note F

5i

 15.   Training the Whistle

This song combines a half note rest and a quarter note rest for three counts of silence.

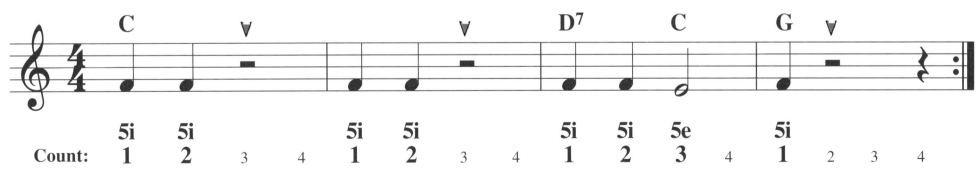

| | C | | | | | | | D⁷ | C | | G | | |

The Trill

The **trill** is a special musical effect.
The trill goes back and forth between a note and its lower neighbour note. Playing a trill is just like shaking your harmonica back and forth while you breathe.

This is how we play a number **4** and **5** hole inhaled trill.
Empty out your lungs. Aim your lips at hole number **5** and inhale.
Continue to inhale and move back so that your lips cover hole number **5** again.
Start out by doing it slowly. Then increase your speed.
Listen to the recorded example and practice.

 16.   A Trillion F's

This is the symbol for a **trill**.

We put the symbol under the **upper note** of the two notes that are to be trilled.
A trill symbol under the half note **5i** means to trill between **5i** and **4i** for two counts.

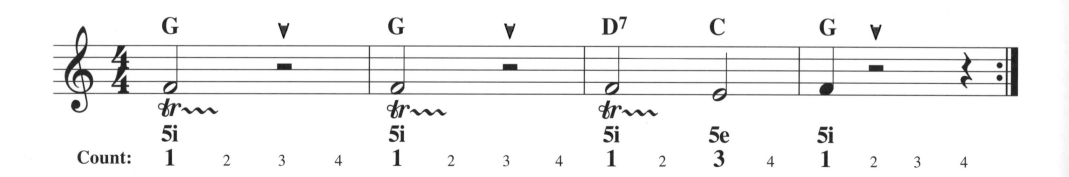

The Dotted Half Note

A dot placed after a half note means that you hold the note for **three** counts.

Count: **1** 2 3

 17.   **Special F-Ect Blues**

This blues style song uses **dotted half notes**. It is eight bars long. Add the trills after you have practiced the song without the trills.

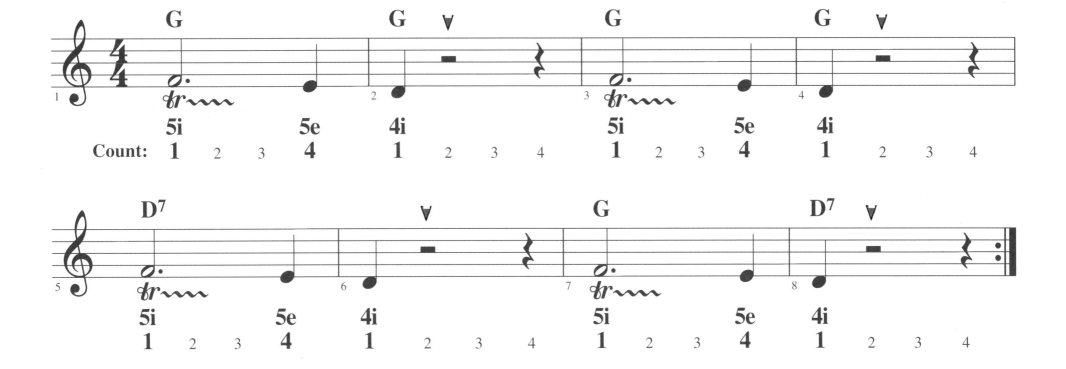

18. Scare-E

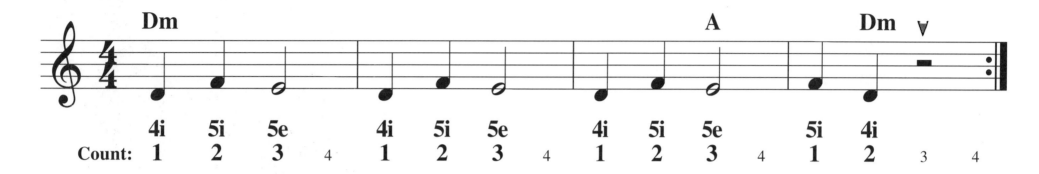

Lesson 7

The Note G

The **G** note of your harmonica is written on the second line of the treble staff. This is what it looks like.

We play the **G** note by exhaling on hole number **6**.

The Note G

6e

19. Geepers Creepers

If you need to, you may take a **very quick breath** in the middle of the third bar.

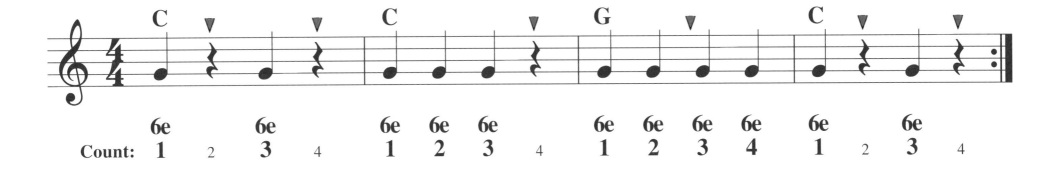

20. Gee-It's Classy

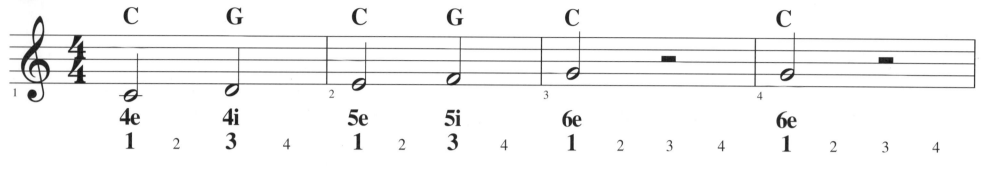

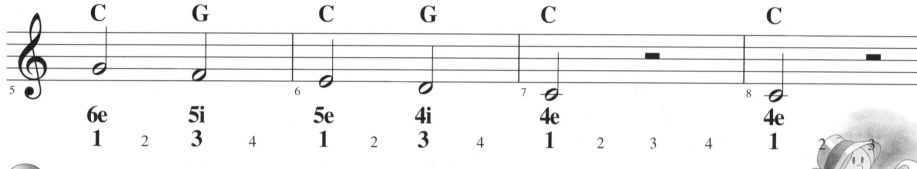

21. Mary Had a Little Lamb

22. Gee-Ups and Downs

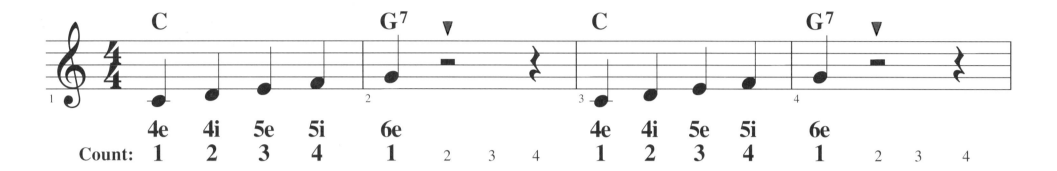

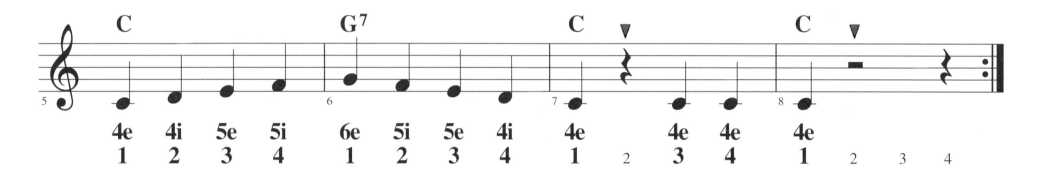

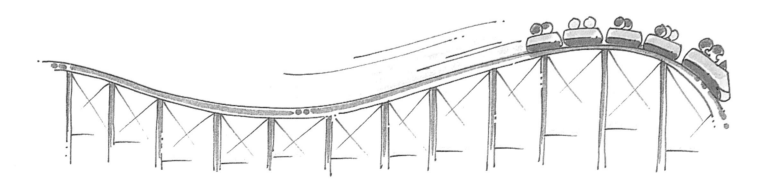

Lesson 8

 23.   Jumpin' Gee

This song will assist you in moving quickly from hole number **4** to hole number **6**.

| Count: | **1** | 2 | **3** | 4 | **1** | 2 | **3** | 4 | **1** | 2 | **3** | 4 | **1** | 2 | 3 | 4 |

4e **6e** **4e** **6e** **4i** **6e** **4e**

 24.   Go Tell Aunt Nancy

Traditional

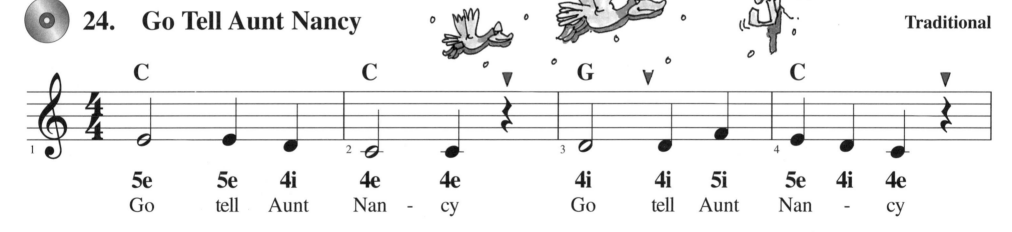

5e   **5e**   **4i**   **4e**   **4e**   **4i**   **4i**   **5i**   **5e**   **4i**   **4e**

Go   tell   Aunt   Nan - cy   Go   tell   Aunt   Nan - cy

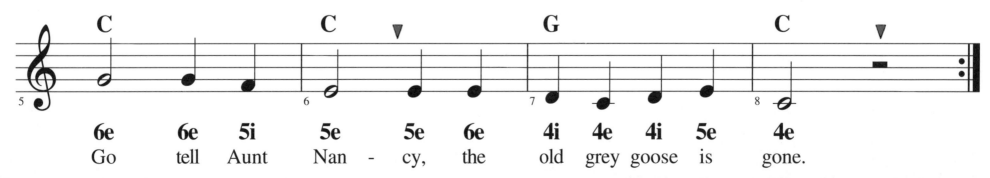

6e   **6e**   **5i**   **5e**   **5e**   **6e**   **4i**   **4e**   **4i**   **5e**   **4e**

Go   tell   Aunt   Nan - cy,   the   old   grey   goose   is   gone.

25. Aura Lee

F   G⁷   C   F

4e 5i 5e 5i 6e 4i 6e 5i 5e 4i 5e 5i

As the black- bird in the spring 'neath the wil - low tree,

F   G⁷   C   F

4e 5i 5e 5i 6e 4i 6e 5i 5e 4i 5e 5i

sat and piped I heard him sing sing of Au - ra Lee.

Staccato

A dot placed **below** or **above** a note tells you to play the note **staccato**. Staccato means to play the note short and separate from other notes. To play a note staccato, use your tongue and whisper a **ta** or **da** sound through your harmonica.

26. It's Staccato!

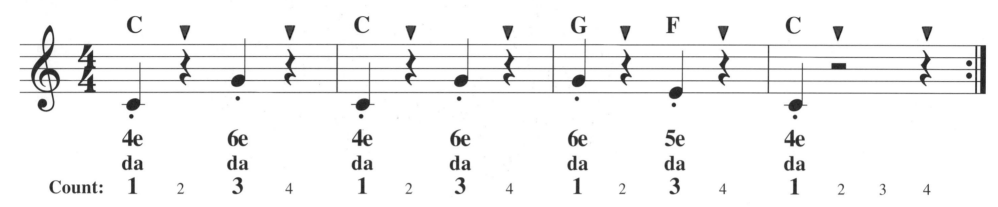

Playing Chords on Purpose

By now you may be able to get single holes easily.
Maybe you are still sometimes playing chords by accident.
Sometimes we play chords on purpose. This is how chords are written.
To play this chord, cover the holes number **4, 5** and **6** and **exhale**.

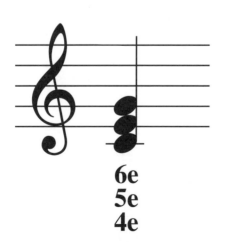

27. Oats and Beans

In this song you will use chords in the **first** and **seventh** bars. Be ready to pucker your lips when you change from a chord to a note.

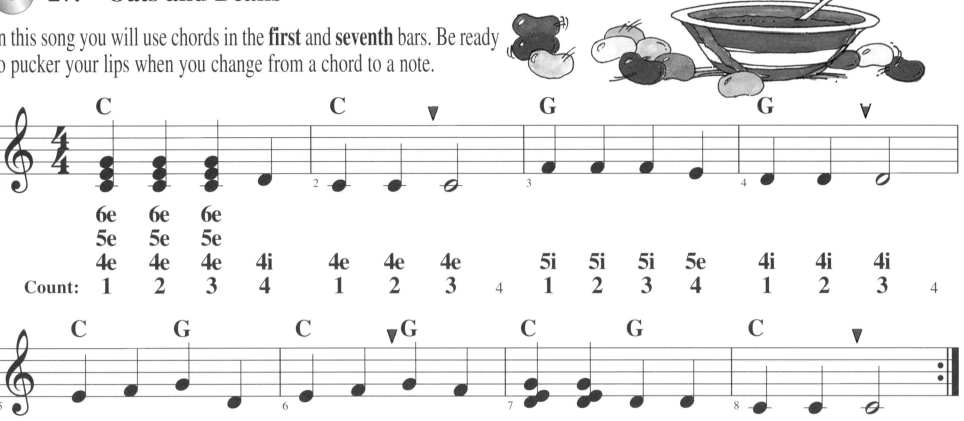

Changing from a chord to a single note can be difficult. Play this song slowly until you can do it accurately.

The Common Time Signature

This symbol is called common time.
It means exactly the same as $\frac{4}{4}$.

28. Lightly Row   **Traditional**

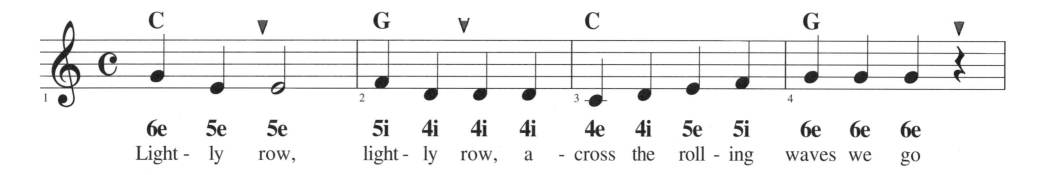

6e   5e   5e   5i   4i   4i   4i   4e   4i   5e   5i   6e   6e   6e
Light - ly row,   light - ly row, a - cross the roll - ing waves we go

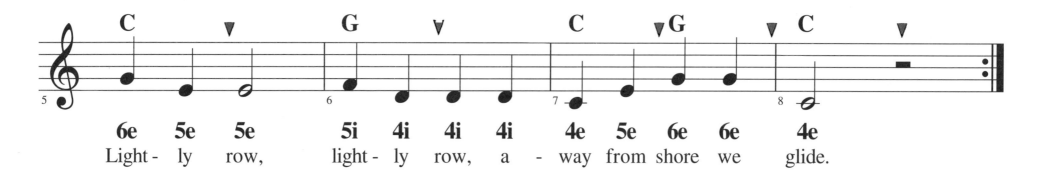

6e   5e   5e   5i   4i   4i   4i   4e   5e   6e   6e   4e
Light - ly row,   light - ly row, a - way from shore we   glide.

Lesson 9

The Three Four Time Signature

The ¾ time signature tells you when there are **three** counts in each bar.
Waltz music is in ¾ time.

 29.   May I Have the First Waltz?

On the recording there are **three** drumbeats to introduce each song in ¾ time.

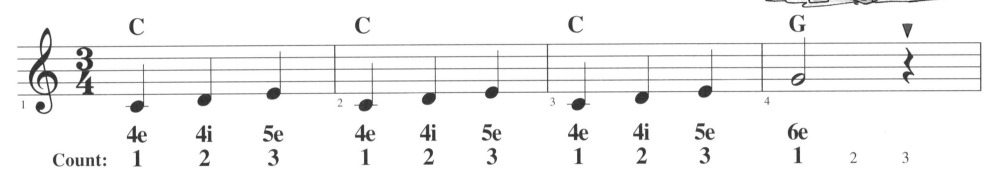

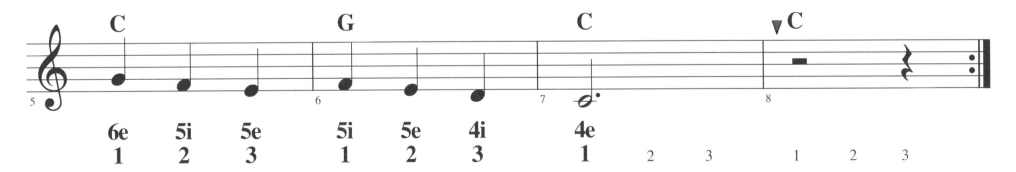

When to Breathe

By this time, you are getting used to taking a breath when necessary.
Unless a song has very difficult breath requirements, no breath symbols will appear.

30. **Austrian Waltz**

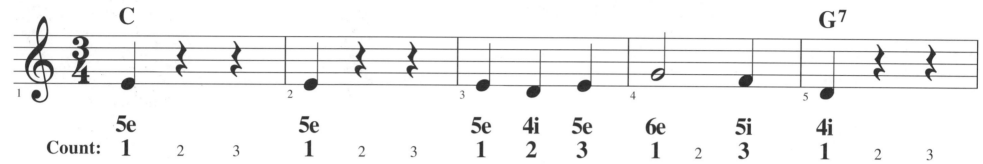

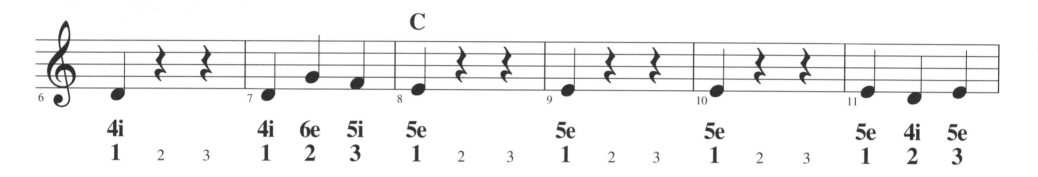

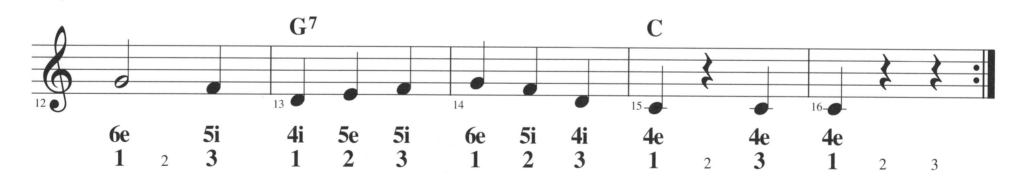

31. Boating Song

Jacques Offenbach

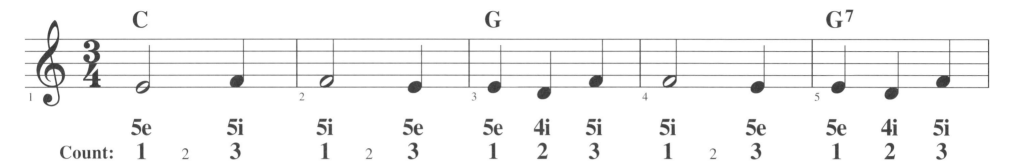

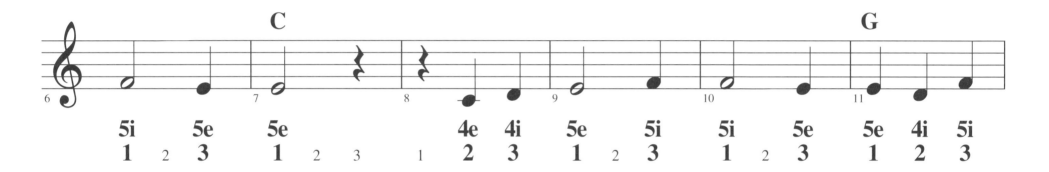

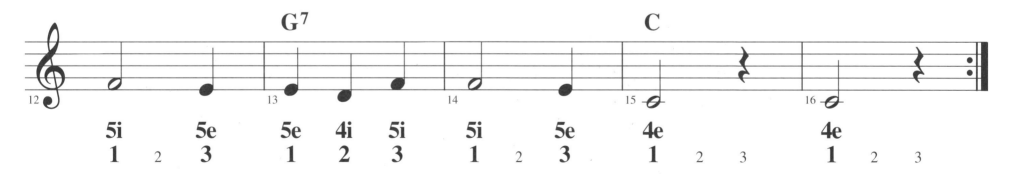

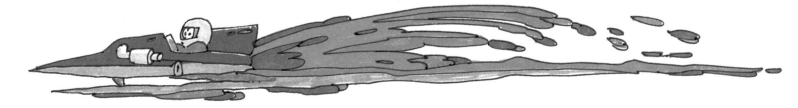

32. Girls and Boys Come Out to Play

Traditional

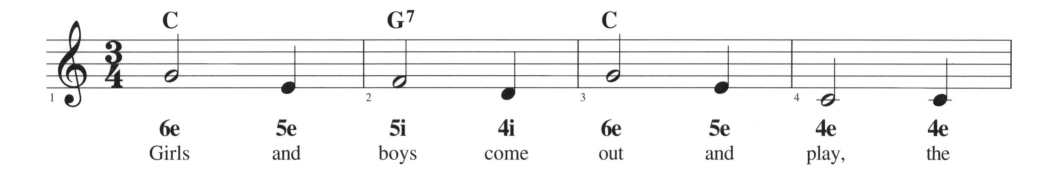

C   **G⁷**   **C**

6e	5e	5i	4i	6e	5e	4e	4e
Girls	and	boys	come	out	and	play,	the

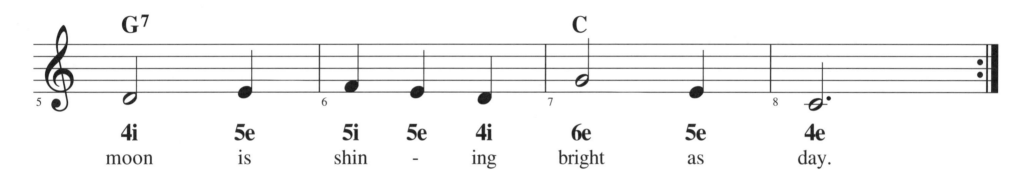

G⁷   **C**

4i	5e	5i	5e	4i	6e	5e	4e
moon	is	shin	-	ing	bright	as	day.

Lesson 10

The Hand Tremolo

The **hand tremolo** adds an interesting sound effect. It is mostly used on longer notes. This is its symbol.

How to Play a Hand Tremolo

Hold your harmonica correctly in our left hand. You may want to review the information page 5.

When you hold your harmonica in this way, a **cup** is formed around the harmonica by the palm and fingers of your left hand.
Now use your right palm to cover the **cup** formed by your left hand.

Keeping the heels of your hand together, open and close the **cup** while you play.

You will hear the tone of the note change. You can open and close the **cup** slowly or rapidly.

 33. Hand Tremolo

34. Trembling Hands

In this song, the hand tremolo is fast and continuous during the half notes.

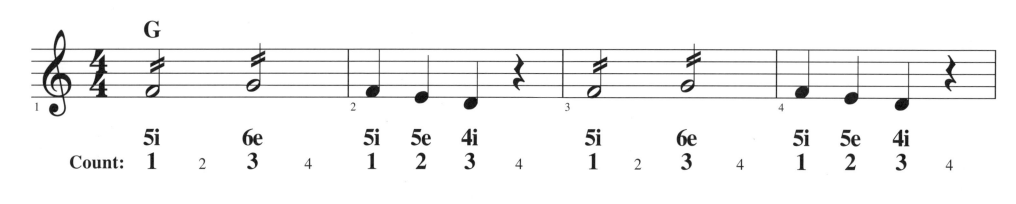

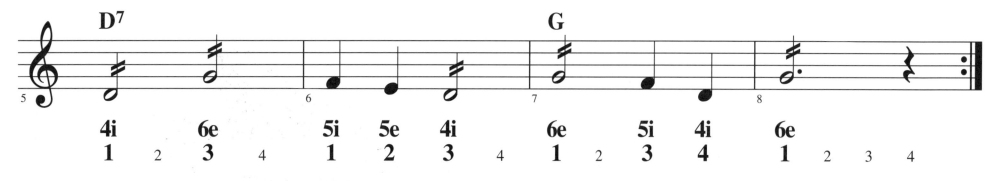

35. Roses from the South

Johann Strauss

Use the hand tremolo effect during **any** of the dotted half notes of this 32 bar song.

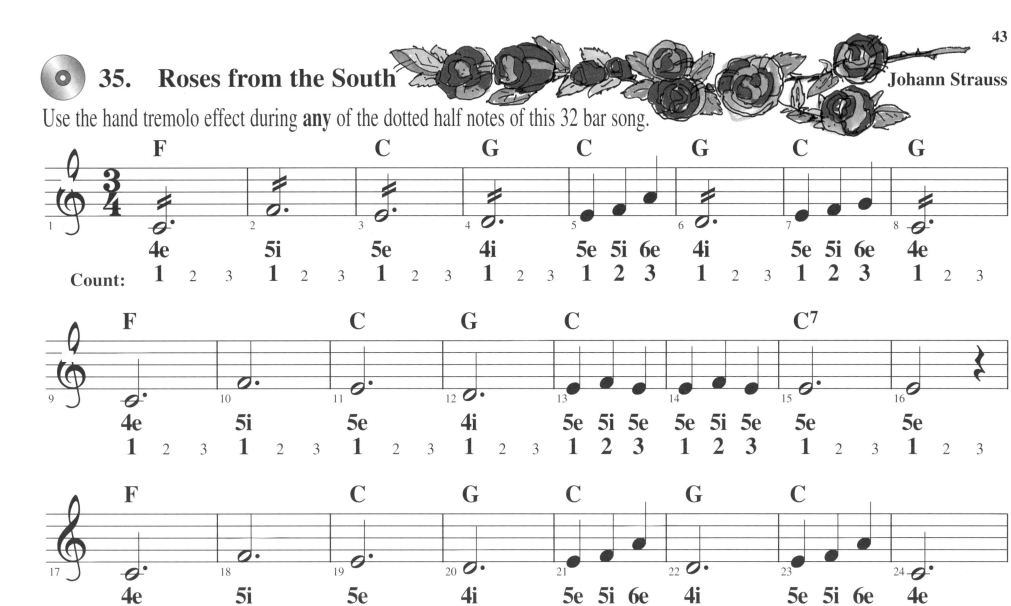

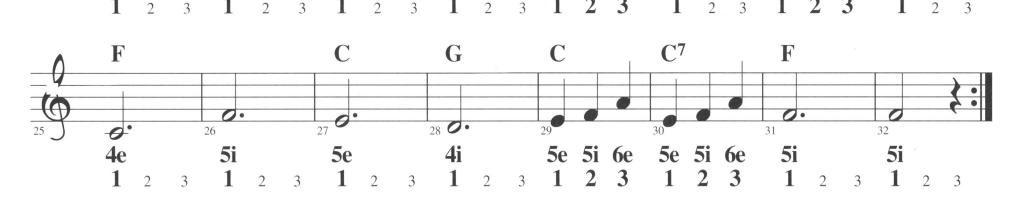

36. **Ode to Joy**

Ludwig Van Beethoven

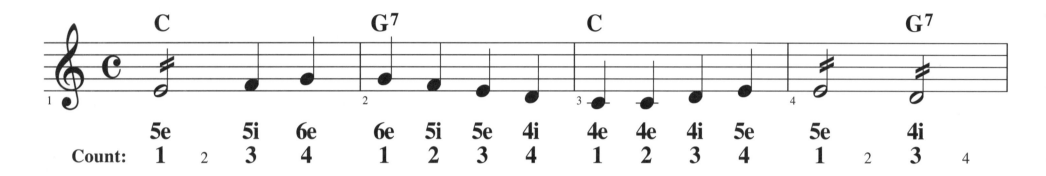

	C				G⁷				C				G⁷	

Note markings: 5e, 5i, 6e, 6e, 5i, 5e, 4i, 4e, 4e, 4i, 5e, 5e, 4i

Count: 1, 2, 3, 4, 1, 2, 3, 4, 1, 2, 3, 4, 1, 2, 3, 4

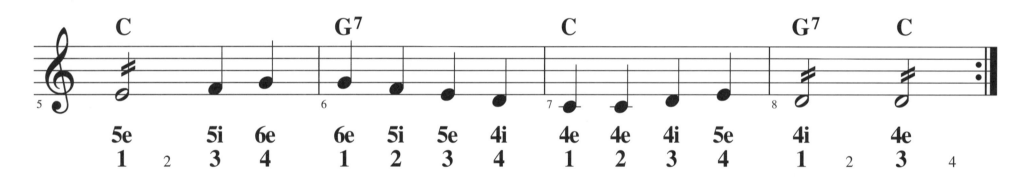

	C				G⁷				C				G⁷	C

Note markings: 5e, 5i, 6e, 6e, 5i, 5e, 4i, 4e, 4e, 4i, 5e, 4i, 4e

Count: 1, 2, 3, 4, 1, 2, 3, 4, 1, 2, 3, 4, 1, 2, 3, 4

Lesson 11

The Whole Note

Count: 1 2 3 4

This is **whole note**.
It last for **four** counts.
There is one whole note in one bar of $\frac{4}{4}$ time.

The Whole Rest

Count: 1 2 3 4

A black box under the middle line of a staff is called a **whole rest**.
It means **four** counts of silence.

The Lead-In (or Pickup)

Sometimes a song does not begin on the first beat of a bar. Any notes which come before the first full bar are called **lead-in notes** (or **pickup notes**).
When we use lead-in notes, the last bar is also incomplete.
The notes of the lead-in and the notes in the last bar add up to one full bar.

37. Gee - It's So Long!

In this song there are two lead-in notes. **Six** drumbeats introduce this song. Add hand tremolo to the long notes.

38. The Banks of the Ohio

Traditional

On the recording, **five** drumbeats introduce this song. Add hand tremolo as you wish.

F

5i
flow,

4e 4e 4i
down by the

5e 5e
banks of

C

G⁷

4i 4i 4i 4e
the O - hi - o.

C⁷

39. Oh When the Saints Go Marchin' In   **Traditional**

On the recording, there are **five** drumbeats to introduce this song.

C

4e 5e 5i 6e
Count: 1 2 3 4 1 O when the Saints

4e 5e 5i 6e
go march-in' in.

4e 5e 5i
O when the

G⁷

C

6e 5e
Saints go

4e 5e
march- in'

4i
in.

5e 5e 4i 4e
O Lord I want to

4e 5e 6e 6e
be in that

F   **Fm**

C   **F**   **G⁷**   **C**

6e 5i
num- ber,

5e 5i 6e 5e
when the Saints go

4e 4i 4e
march - in' in.

The Note Middle C

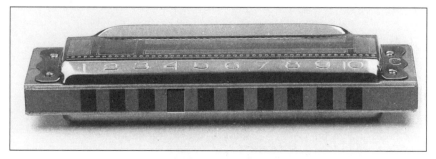

The note **C** is played by breathing **out** through the **fourth** hole.

The Note D

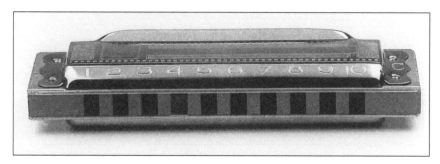

The note **D** is played by breathing **in** through the **fourth** hole.

The Note E

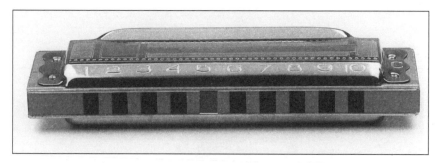

The note **E** is played by breathing **out** through the **fifth** hole.

The Note F

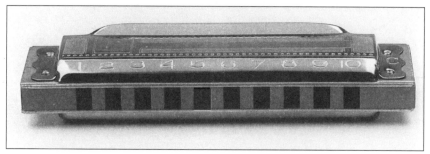

The note **F** is played by breathing **in** through the **fifth** hole.

The Note G

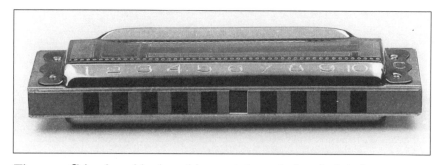

The note **G** is played by breathing **out** through the **sixth** hole.